The Panthéon

Anne **Muratori-Philip**

ÉDITIONS DU PATRIMOINE

CENTRE DES
MONUMENTS NATIONAUX

30 November 2002. Night had fallen when five riders appeared in front of the Panthéon: an immaculate Marianne, symbol of the French Republic, followed by four musketeers. The crowd was emotional. Silent, it watched out for the arrival of the coffin of Alexandre Dumas, borne by pall-bearers. Around 8 p.m., the door of the monument closed on the writer for eternity. And the musketeers went back down the Rue Soufflot to an immense ovation. One hundred and seventeen years previously, on 1 June 1885, the same fervour had marked the funeral of Victor Hugo. The heart of Paris had stopped beating when the immense catafalque draped in black drew up to the Panthéon.

Many other inhumations have marked the history of the monument, including Voltaire in 1791, Jean-Jacques Rousseau in 1794, Émile Zola in 1908, Jean Jaurès in 1924, Victor Schoelcher in 1949, and Jean Moulin in 1964. Not to mention the entry of Marie Curie in 1995. All of Europe had gathered together to pay homage to the only woman welcomed for her achievements.

On the Montagne Sainte-Geneviève

"A grateful nation honours its great men": the Panthéon today bears its inscription with such pride that it has ended up forgetting its long history—sometimes glorious, but often turbulent.

Its foundations date to 496, when Clovis, who had just been baptised, decided to build a royal basilica on a Paris hill located next to the former Gallo-Roman forum of Lutetia. The king of the Franks had Geneviève, the patron saint of Paris, buried in the crypt. From the 6th century, her tomb became a site of pilgrimage. The basilica then took the name of Saint Geneviève and the hill, in the heart of the present Latin Quarter, became the Montagne Sainte-Geneviève. In 857 the basilica was sacked by Norman invaders. Fortunately, the shrine containing the saint's relics escaped unscathed.

Sainte-Geneviève served as a model for churches such as Saint Isaac's in Saint Petersburg, as well as for civil buildings such as the Capitol in Washington and the Capitol in Sacramento.

Introduction

Rebuilt in the 12th century, the basilica threatened to fall into ruin from the 17th century. A renovation was in order, but funds were lacking. For a century, the monks did their best to preserve the building, not imagining that a saviour would come to their aid. And yet, this unexpected saviour existed—he was the most powerful man in the kingdom.

1744: The vow of Louis XV

On 8 August 1744, during the War of the Austrian Succession, Louis XV fell seriously ill in Metz. For ten dreadful days, his entourage thought there was no hope for him. Then a miracle took place, and the king got better. Around the country, the news of his recovery prompted outbursts of joy. Upon returning from the war, Louis XV made his entry into Paris accompanied by illuminations and fireworks. Homages, harangues, and *Te Deums* followed one another. The grand finale was his act of thanksgiving to Saint Geneviève on 17 November 1744. On that occasion, the king promised the *génovéfains*—the canons regular of the abbey of Sainte-Geneviève—that the dilapidated sanctuary would be rebuilt.

After the royal vow, ten years went by. Had the promise been forgotten? Fortunately for the basilica, the politico-religious affairs rocking the kingdom obliged Louis XV to react. To strengthen his image, he intended to deliver a political message to his subjects through the arts: this was the announcement on 9 December 1754 that the church of Sainte-Geneviève would be rebuilt. The king thus reminded his subjects that he was the sole depositary of the divine right of kings.

Soufflot's bold plan

The salvaging of the basilica began immediately. In January 1755, Louis XV entrusted the task to Jacques Germain Soufflot, a Burgundian architect whose audacity and inventiveness were praised.

To endow his work with more light and splendour, the architect envisaged combining Greek plan and Gothic structure. His plan: to erect a "functional" church, centred on the reliquary of Saint Geneviève. But, as a man of the Enlightenment, he also shared the ideas of Diderot who hoped that "the purpose of a building was guessed as soon as it was in sight".

Two years later, on 2 March 1757, Louis XV approved the project. Inspired by Saint Peter's Basilica in Rome, Soufflot devised a centralised plan, in the form of a Greek cross with four arms of equal length, in which the nave was preceded by a temple portico in the colossal Corinthian order, crowned with a pediment. A lantern-tower, or dome with two cupolas, rose above the transept crossing—where the shrine containing the saint's relics, supported by four caryatids representing the cardinal virtues, was to have pride of place. For all eyes to be attracted to this jewel, the number of masonry pillars and thick arcades had to be limited. As for the central dome, it was designed to rest on four shallow triangular piers, whose corner columns aligned with those of the nave and choir. Each arm of the cross was to be covered with a vault supported by pendentives, in between two barrel vaults, which were to emerge from the avant-corps of the interior colonnade. To contain the thrust of the vaults, flying buttresses, concealed behind the attic storey of the façades, were to support the building. Finally, the structure of the church was to be reinforced by the systematic use of the "reinforced stone" technique, which consisted in fastening the stone blocs together using a metal framework. The light was to enter through a clever blend of side and oblique structures, as well as forty-two large windows encircling the sanctuary.

Cutting criticisms and royal support

From the outset of construction, Soufflot's innovations provoked criticisms on the part of the Church, which deemed his project too bold. In 1758 the architect took up his working diagram again with a view to meeting liturgical demands. He broke the harmony of the Greek cross by extending the eastern arm with a choir, with two towers at its chevet. Then he added a narthex to the west.

Other difficulties awaited the architect, such as the discovery of sixty-nine clay quarry pits dating to the Gallo-Roman period. They had to be filled in and the initial plan put right by reinforcing the foundations. This unforeseen change accounts for the size of the crypt. It far surpassed the needs of the *génovéfains*, whose community comprised no more than thirty-four members on the eve of the French Revolution.

In 1763, as soon as the crypt was finished, Soufflot got the king to agree to visit the building site. He suggested that Louis XV himself lay the foundation stone of the building, which had barely begun to rise from the ground. With this ritual gesture, the king evoked his vow of 1744 and demonstrated his attachment to the progress of the arts, while strengthening Soufflot's position, which was aggressively contested by his peers.

On 6 September 1764, at 11 a.m., Louis XV and the dauphin took their places on a gigantic stage set flanked by imposing stands where Parisians had thronged to get seats a few hours earlier. Impressed, the king then discovered the façade of the new abbey church in life-size, painted in perspective on canvas-covered stretchers, attached to a frame that would later serve as scaffolding for the building works. A provisional pavement circumscribed the sanctuary where the sovereign, silver-gilt trowel in hand, laid the foundation stone. The scene was immortalised by Pierre Antoine De Machy in a painting entitled *Louis XV Lays the Foundation Stone for the New Church of Sainte-Geneviève, 6 September 1764*. Realism guaranteed—the artist also executed the *trompe-l'oeil* model of the church.

Confident of royal support, Soufflot pursued his work. But the changes imposed by the ecclesiastics obliged him to reconsider the plans for the dome. An arduous task, as evidenced by the five unsuccessful projects. In 1777 he finally finished the definitive plan. In the meantime, the architect Pierre Patte, who had liked Soufflot's initial projects, had made an about-turn. According to Patte, the supports planned for the corners of the transept crossing were inadequate to bear the weight of the dome.

Louis XV Lays the Foundation Stone for the New Church of Sainte-Geneviève, 6 September 1764 by Pierre Antoine De Machy, oil on canvas (Musée Carnavalet, Paris).

Section of the crossing designed by the architect Brébion according to the dying wishes of Soufflot, 1780 (MAP, Charenton-le-Pont).

Executed between 1783 and 1787 by the architect Jean-Baptiste Rondelet, this model was presented to Louis XVI and Marie-Antoinette. The section reveals the three superposed stone calottes that make up the dome.

An impressive 83-metre dome

After the death of Louis XV in 1774, the colonnades of the nave and peristyle were finished, but the building project made little headway due to lack of funding. Fortunately, Soufflot managed to interest Louis XVI and Marie-Antoinette in the project by presenting them with a very flattering model. And so construction started once again.

In 1778 a few cracks in the drums of the crossing rekindled Patte's fury. Despite a reassuring expert's report, the debate continued, especially as the press regularly fanned the flames. It came to an end on 29 August 1780, with the sudden death of the unfortunate Soufflot, who had just finished the roofing of the naves.

Louis XVI appointed Maximilien Brébion as his successor. Soufflot's close collaborator, Brébion kept the same loyal team. The team included the architect's nephew, known as Soufflot le

Romain, and Jean-Baptiste Rondelet, a young engineer from Lyon who had helped Soufflot with his daring ideas.

While the decorations of the pediment (*The Adoration of the Cross* by Guillaume Coustou II) and peristyle (the lives of Saint Geneviève, Saint Peter, and Saint Paul) were taking shape, the team began building the dome. Finished in 1790, it rests on an immense drum, decorated on the exterior with thirty-two columns and pierced on the interior with two rows of windows. These are topped with three superposed stone calottes. The first cupola, whose centre is hollowed out, allows a second cupola, 60 metres high, to be seen. Decorated by Gros, it is lit by a row of windows that is completely invisible from the interior. The third cupola supports a lantern that reaches 83 metres at its highest point.

Certainly, Rondelet embedded in the masonry a network of iron rods that had not been planned for, but the three stone calottes that fitted together perfectly represented a posthumous victory for Soufflot.

1790: The clergy makes way for the Pantheon

Just as the dome was taking shape, the kingdom was in turmoil. In the church of Sainte-Geneviève, one ran into painters, sculptors, and ornamentists more worried about their future than about the execution of the decorations for the interior. The church had not yet been consecrated—and never would be! The nationalisation of Church property, promulgated on 2 November 1789, then the abolition of religious orders on 13 February 1790, would allow the Constituent Assembly to twist Soufflot's masterpiece to serve patriotism in search of sacredness.

The idea of transforming the church into a "pantheon" of illustrious men was launched. We owe it to Marquis Charles de Villette, who insisted on obtaining a Parisian tomb for his friend Voltaire. On 30 May 1790, he wrote: "In the tradition of the Greeks and Romans, from whom we have received the maxims of liberty, and as an example to the rest of Europe, let us have the courage not to dedicate this temple to a saint. Let it become the Pantheon of France! Let us install the statues of our great men and lay their ashes to rest in its underground recesses" (*Le Panthéon, symbole des révolutions*, 98–99).

On this page from a book of drawings executed in Saint-Lazare by Hubert Robert, the painter reminds us that Soufflot's Panthéon is the worthy heir of classical art. Watercolour, *c.* 1794.

View of the interior of the church of Sainte-Geneviève, engraving by Meunier, late 18th century (Musée Carnavalet, Paris). At the transept crossing, the shrine containing the saint's relics is supported by four caryatids representing the cardinal virtues, works by Germain Pilon. The atmosphere of the church was still bright, welcoming, and pristine. This was altered completely when the sanctuary was turned into a Temple of the Nation.

The Panthéon around 1790, by F. J. Belanger (BNF, Paris). The lower windows had not yet been walled up.

While the Panthéon is the offspring of the Revolution, its creation was not an improvisation springing from the wild imaginings of the sans-culottes. It was, on the contrary, the result of half a century of philosophical debate on the invention of a new, secular memorial with which Fénelon, Montesquieu, and Voltaire were not unfamiliar. Rejecting the combative hero, the philosophers of the Enlightenment advocated that a great man should be chosen for his merit. "To achieve great things, there is no need to be such a great genius," wrote Montesquieu. "One must not place oneself above men, but alongside them."

Mirabeau overtakes Voltaire

A powerful orator from the outset, Count Honoré-Gabriel de Mirabeau, who died suddenly on 2 April 1791, was the first to profit from Villette's suggestion. Two days later, the Assembly adopted Marquis Emmanuel de Pastoret's bill to dedicate the new building to the glorious dead. The decree specified that the following would be inscribed on the pediment: "A grateful nation honours its great men." That very evening, after a grandiose funeral, Mirabeau entered the building and was placed in a temporary location.

Meanwhile, Villette continued his crusade to have Voltaire's remains sent back home—the nationalisation of Church property, voted in 1789, threatened them with exhumation. The philosopher had died in Paris on 30 May 1778, and the Church had refused him Christian burial. His nephew Alexandre-Jean Mignot, commendatory abbot of Sellières, near Romilly-sur-Seine, had him secretly buried at the abbey. But with the inevitable sale of the abbey, what would become of the remains of Voltaire?

In 1791 Villette's stubbornness finally won over the members of the Constituent Assembly: Voltaire was to return to Paris with great pomp and ceremony. The transfer of the remains, delayed by the capture of the king, who was fleeing Paris, at Varennes, took place on 11 July. The day before, the coffin left Sellières on a chariot decked with flowers, heading for the ruins of the Bastille, where it spent the night on a cenotaph. The following day, a long, colourful cortège, headed by the cavalry and infantry, preceded the porphyry catafalque. The busts of Mirabeau,

Franklin, and Rousseau led the way, followed by the sappers of the National Guard and the demolishers of the Bastille. Numerous figurants, all in classical dress, marched past. Some of them carried a model of the fortress, others the statue of a seated Voltaire, a replica of the sculpture by Houdon; there was also a chest filled with the philosopher's works. Behind the representatives of the people, a choir sang civic hymns. Twelve white horses pulled the immense chariot, which was 9 metres high, at the top of which appeared a wax figure of the deceased on his death bed and crowned with Glory.

After a stop in front of the Opéra, then another under Villette's windows (on the present Quai Voltaire), and stops at the Café Procope and the Nouvelle-Comédie (now the Théâtre de l'Odéon), the equipage ended its interminable journey in front of the Panthéon at night. By torchlight, Voltaire's coffin was also given a temporary location, next to Mirabeau.

This gigantic civic ceremony was organised by Jacques Louis David. It would serve as a model for all the other "pantheonisations".

Lepeletier and Marat enter, Mirabeau exits

Once the fitting out of the crypt was finished, Mirabeau and Voltaire were laid to rest there, on 13 December 1791. The following year, the reliquary of Saint Geneviève was exiled to the neighbouring church of Saint-Étienne-du-Mont. It was replaced with the mayoral scarf of Jacques Guillaume Simonneau, who was killed by rioters in his city of Étampes on 3 March 1792. The deputy Bertrand Barère de Vieuzac spoke of this unknown person as a "martyr for liberty and faithfulness to the law".

It was not until 24 January 1793 that the first hero of the French Revolution entered the Panthéon: Louis Michel Lepeletier de Saint-Fargeau, deputy for the Yonne at the Convention. After having voted for the death of Louis XVI, he was murdered the following day by one of the king's former bodyguards. But Lepeletier's remains left the monument on 14 February 1795, at his daughter's request.

The Constituent Assembly had initially decided that only great men "from the era of our liberty" could enter the Panthéon. The French Revolution was too young to have great men; as for the martyrs chosen, not all of them had unanimous support. Thus, each faction attempted to get a spot for "its" great man. Jean-Paul Marat, the editor of *L'Ami du peuple* (The Friend of the People) stabbed by Charlotte Corday, received this honour on 21 September 1794. He drove out the remains of Mirabeau, who was declared a traitor to the nation after the discovery of compromising documents in the king's iron chest in the Palais des Tuileries.

That year, David had also planned a "heroic festival" for two young heroes killed in action, Joseph Bara and Agricol Viala. Scheduled for 28 July 1794 (10 Thermidor, Year II), the festival was cancelled after the fall of Robespierre.

In comes Rousseau, out goes Marat

On 11 October 1794, it was Jean-Jacques Rousseau's turn to enter the Panthéon. Like Voltaire, he died in 1778. He was buried on the Île des Peupliers in Ermenonville, the estate of the Marquis of Girardin, his patron and disciple.

Having entered Paris on the evening of 10 October, the coffin spent the night in the ornamental lake of the Tuileries, on a mound representing the Île des Peupliers. The next day, the classical-style cortège that crossed Paris resembled that of Voltaire. All along the coffin's route, the public sang arias from *Le Devin du village* (The Village Soothsayer), Rousseau's only opera. The flags of the French, Genevan, and American republics headed the procession, followed by the orphans of the Defenders of the Nation. The Institut National de Musique preceded the Convention deputies, who were in groups behind an immense copy of *Le Contrat social* (The Social Contract). The funeral chariot carrying a statue of Rousseau sitting in the shade of a tree, a child at his knee, slowly made its way to the Panthéon.

Marat's presence near Rousseau soon appeared to be an "irreparable sacrilege". It was even claimed that, if Marat remained in place, the temple would fall down! The anti-Jacobin days of February 1795 were fateful. Shortly afterwards, Marat's remains discreetly left the Panthéon.

Relieved, Louis-Sébastien Mercier wrote at the time: "Let us be wary of pantheonising rashly because we should no longer worship idols. The Panthéon has already been sullied twice" (*Le Nouveau Paris*, book VI, 873). To avoid further blunders, the Convention then decided to have the glorious dead wait

ten long years before perhaps bestowing the honours of the Panthéon upon them.

Towards a sombre and austere monument

For the time being, a lot of work remained to be done on the former basilica. The task was entrusted to Antoine Chrysostome Quatremère de Quincy on 19 July 1791. The new project supervisor was not an architect, but a sculptor passionate about classical antiquity. To transform the building into a cenotaph for great men and Temple of the Nation, he had the good sense to make Rondelet and Soufflot le Romain part of his team.

Quatremère de Quincy toned down Soufflot's work, deemed too bright, in order to confer on it an austere solemnity. He wanted the building to have the shadowy light of classical temples. The thirty-nine lower windows that brought light into the nave and the transept were thus bricked up. By fitting out the upper windows with frosted glass, he obtained gloomy and mysterious top lighting that was appropriate for a mausoleum. The exterior of the monument with its blind façades, punctuated by the garlands of the frieze retained by Quatremère de Quincy,

Just after the fall of Robespierre, the transfer of Jean-Jacques Rousseau's ashes gave rise to a grand celebration; a classical-style cortège preceded the statue of the philosopher sitting under a tree. Moitte's pediment to the glory of the nation, which was finished the previous year, is depicted on the engraving (private collection, Paris).

took on an unusual appearance. The religious attributes vanished in turn: the two small bell towers of the chevet, the lantern topping the dome, and the religious sculptures of the pediment and peristyle were removed. Two hundred workers hunted down fleurs-de-lis, the medallions of Louis XV and Louis XVI, and religious symbols, as well as rinceaux and rosettes. "Useless puerilities", according to Quatremère de Quincy.

Quatremère de Quincy worked out a patriotic decorative scheme in which sculpture was given the lion's share. On the pediment, *The Adoration of the Cross* by Coustou gave way, from 1793, to *The Nation Crowning Civic and Martial Virtues*, sculpted by Jean Guillaume Moitte. He replaced the five religious bas-reliefs of the peristyle with *The Declaration of the Rights of Man* by Guillaume Boichot, *The Empire of Faith* by Fortin, *The New Jurisprudence* by Roland, *Patriotic Devotion* by Antoine-Denis Chaudet, and *State Education* by Jean-Philippe Lesueur. These works were removed during the Restoration; then, in 1833, Chaudet and Lesueur's sculptures were returned to their places, where they can be seen to this day.

Inside, Quatremère de Quincy took advantage of the cross-shaped plan of the building to assign an allegorical theme to each nave: philosophy, the sciences, the arts, and patriotism. Finally, from Claude Dejoux he commissioned a 9-metre-high statue of Fame to crown the dome. But this messenger of glory was never hoisted to the top: in March 1794, construction ground to a halt after Quatremère de Quincy was arrested. The unfortunate man had paid the price for the views he expressed as deputy for Paris at the Legislative Assembly.

Garland of laurel and oak leaves encircling the tops of the blind façades, testimony to the exterior decoration designed by Soufflot.

Saved by Bonaparte, who returns it to the Church

In December 1795, new cracks appeared in the piers of the crossing. And the inexhaustible Pierre Patte rekindled the controversy. An initial committee of experts, made up of Rondelet, Jean-François Chalgrin, Alexandre-Théodore Brongniart, and Gondouin, examined the building on 8 Ventôse, Year IV (27 February 1796). It handed in an alarming report. But no one agreed on the remedies to be taken. Expert's report after expert's report, the dispute raged on. Meanwhile, Rondelet decided to brace the four piers with masonry and timber centring, which he himself found ghastly.

On 24 December 1799, Napoleon Bonaparte became first consul. He inherited a Panthéon cluttered with the struts that were the despair of Rondelet, from then on the sole architect in charge of the building. On 15 July 1801, the signing of the Concordat with Pope Pius VII brought an end to the schism that had divided the Church of France since the Revolution. Its terms included the reopening of places of worship.

Rondelet did not know it at the time, but the Concordat was to save his dear Panthéon. Emperor since 18 May 1804, Napoleon realised that consecrating and restoring the former basilica of Sainte-Geneviève (and that of Saint-Denis) could be associated with the expedient act of atoning for the regicide. On 13 February 1806, he visited the building in the company of Rondelet and asked him thousands of questions. Disorientated, Rondelet got tangled up in confused explanations. Fortunately, Pierre François Fontaine, the emperor's favourite architect, defended his colleague's project. Convinced, the emperor allocated 500,000 francs for the construction works, which began immediately with the bracing of the piers. Six year later, the scaffolding was taken down, enabling Soufflot's dome to be admired at long last.

On 20 February 1806, the emperor signed the decree that made the Panthéon a place of worship once again, while specifying that the crypt would retain the civic function assigned to the building in 1791. The church once again became that of Sainte-Geneviève. It was served by six canons from the chapter of Notre-Dame, who officiated during the state funerals of imperial dignitaries and the main religious holidays. They also went to celebrate the anniversaries and prominent events of the reign—such as the feast day of Saint Napoleon!

The imperial ceremonial necessitated changes to the church and the crypt. Between 1806 and 1809, the laying of a magnificent pavement put the finishing touches to the work of Soufflot. The choir was given stalls for the chapter of canons, as well as a large raised altar. Other altars were planned for the ends of the transept, and sacristies were built.

Grand mausoleum of the dignitaries of the Empire

Between 1809 and 1811, major changes were made to the crypt. Rondelet provided a separate entrance for the church when he built the east porch, which opened onto an Imperial staircase. Two hundred and forty-two recesses were fitted out to contain the remains of the "grand dignitaries, grand officers of the Empire, senators, and citizens for services rendered to the nation". Rondelet had even prepared in advance sarcophagi adorned with inscriptions and decorated with stars, eagles, and the cross of the Legion of Honour. As required by the Concordat, a space (vault IV) was provided for Protestants. Finally, the older church of Sainte-Geneviève was demolished, which enabled space to be cleared around the monument, the Rue Soufflot to be widened, and new streets, such as the Rue d'Ulm and the Rue Clovis, to be created.

During the Empire, forty-two dignitaries were given the honour of being interred in the crypt. The lawyer François Denis Tronchet entered first, on 17 March 1806. The counsel for Louis XVI, he took part in the drafting of the Civil Code along with Jean Portalis, Jean-Baptiste Treilhard, and Claude Régnier, who later joined him in the Panthéon. Nineteen soldiers of the Napoleonic epic were interred there, including Marshal Lannes, nicknamed "Roland of the Army". In addition to twenty-seven senators and a few clergymen, including Cardinal Giovanni Battista Caprara, who presided over the signing of the Concordat, the crypt also received the navigator Louis Antoine de Bougainville; the doctor Pierre Jean Georges Cabanis; Emmanuel Crétet, the first governor of the Banque de France; and Joseph-Marie Vien, the first artist to be interred in the Panthéon.

On 9 August 1811, Antoine Jean Gros received the commission for the painting for the cupola; he was given eighteen months to execute the project. The artist took up the theme chosen by Soufflot, *The Apotheosis of Saint Geneviève*, but adapted it to suit the Empire. He thus sketched "a glory of angels carrying the reliquary of Saint Geneviève up to heaven". They were surrounded by Clovis and Clotilde, founders of the first church; Charlemagne; Saint Louis; and the imperial couple Napoleon 1 and Marie-Louise dedicating the new church to the saint.

The fall of the Empire in 1814 hampered the momentum, all the more so as Gros had fallen behind in his work: only the groups featuring Clovis and Charlemagne were completed.

Keeping a low profile during the Restoration

In the days following the abdication of Napoleon, Louis XVIII moved into the Palais des Tuileries. It was the ambition of Louis Pierre Baltard, who had succeeded Rondelet in 1813, to restructure Soufflot's work. In actual fact, he contented himself with getting rid of the Napoleonic adornments, initials, and symbols. In the edict of 12 April 1816, Louis XVIII returned the basilica of Sainte-Geneviève to Catholic worship and placed it under the authority of the archbishop of Paris. To illustrate this new religious policy, the king attended the consecration ceremony of the

Detail of the cupola painted by Gros (1811–24). Louis XVIII and his niece, the duchess of Angoulême. While an angel brandishes the constitutional charter, the work of the king, the duchess raises her eyes to the heavens where her parents, Louis XVI and Marie-Antoinette, rest.

church on 3 January 1822. The saint's reliquary was even returned to its place. Destroyed in 1793, it was recreated thanks to a few relics saved from the iconoclastic fury.

In charge of its church once again, the clergy was none too pleased at the cohabitation of the saint with the remains of Voltaire and Rousseau. It found a compromise, exiling the atheist philosophers to an invisible corner of the crypt, locked behind a gate. As for the Bourbons, they were not in favour of the pantheonisations. They only made one exception to respect the wishes of the *génovéfains*, authorising the interment of Soufflot on 19 February 1829. It was just a question of making it official since the remains of the architect had been waiting for this homage for forty-nine years.

Under Louis XVIII, then Charles X, major changes were made to the decoration of the building. A crossed topped the dome, while the pediment inscription became *"D.O.M. sub. invocat. S. Genovafae. Lud. XV. dicavit. Lud. XVIII. restituit"*. The pediment itself, sculpted by Moitte and hidden by tarpaulins since 1816, was destroyed in 1823. Baltard replaced it with a radiant cross. The artist François Gérard painted allegories of Justice, Death, the Nation, and Fame on the pendentives supporting the dome. As for Gros, he was asked to finish the decoration of the cupola by replacing Napoleon and Marie-Louise with portraits of Louis XVIII and his niece, the pious duchess of Angoulême. Louis XVI and Marie-Antoinette also made an appearance, according to the wishes of Louis XVIII, who was preoccupied with reminding people of his legitimacy.

1830: The clergy departs once again

The Revolution of 1830 swept Charles X out of power after *Les Trois Glorieuses*, the three days of fighting in July that gave their name to the new monarchy. His cousin the duke of Orléans became king of the French. Unlike the Restoration, the July Monarchy sought to become deeply rooted in a form of national legitimacy, heir to both the *Ancien Régime* and the Revolution. But, fundamentally anticlerical, the new government wanted the Church to have nothing to do with the State. On 26 August 1830, Louis-Philippe I hastened to return the Panthéon to "its original and legal purpose. . . . The inscription

'A grateful nation honours its great men' will be restored to the pediment and the remains of Great Men will be laid to rest there". The relics of Saint Geneviève went into exile again and the cross topping the dome was taken down. The painter Gérard finished the pendentives commissioned during the Restoration; the only change was that *Fame* was transformed into *Glory*. And the remains of Voltaire and Rousseau returned to their initial locations in the vestibule of the crypt.

Then the Panthéon fell asleep, left out of the artistic policies of Louis-Philippe's ministers. The only major commission by the July Monarchy concerned the pediment and peristyle decorations. On the pediment, the religious bas-relief by Baltard made way for a large composition by David d'Angers: *The Nation Distributing Crowns Handed to Her by Liberty to Great Men, Civil and Military, While History Inscribes Their Name*. Charles François Leboeuf, known as Nanteuil, executed three bas-reliefs for the peristyle: *The Apotheosis of the Hero Who Died for His Country, The Judicature*, and *The Sciences and the Arts*.

During his reign, Louis-Philippe organised only one event at the Panthéon, on 29 July 1831, on the occasion of the first anniversary of *Les Trois Glorieuses*. To the sounds of "La Marseillaise", he paid homage to the combatants of July by symbolically sealing four bronze tablets engraved with the victims' names. Then, the Panthéon once again languished in obscurity for seventeen years.

1851: Return of the clergy—for the third time

In February 1848, the Second Republic succeeded the July Monarchy. In the euphoria of victory, the provisional government envisaged making the Panthéon a "Temple of Humanity". But the enthusiasm quickly waned. For a few months, the physicist Léon Foucault made use of the dome to demonstrate the Earth's rotation using the pendulum that made him famous. The experiment ended on 1 December 1851.

The following day, the anniversary of the victory of Austerlitz and of the coronation of Napoleon I, Louis Napoleon Bonaparte, the prince-president, carried out a coup d'état. As a precautionary measure, the Panthéon was closed.

On 6 December 1851, Louis Napoleon went back to the starting point, promulgating the following decree: "The former church of Sainte-Geneviève is once again a place of worship, in accordance with the wishes of its founder, under the protection of Saint Geneviève, patron saint of Paris." Elevated to the rank of national basilica, it was henceforth served by a chapter of canons whose dean was appointed by Emperor Napoleon III and the archbishop of Paris. Simon Claude Constant-Dufeux, the new architect, improvised makeshift altars, and installed a pulpit and stalls in anticipation of its inauguration on 3 January 1853. On 21 January, the reliquary of Saint Geneviève was returned to its place underneath the dome. A umpteenth twist in the saga of the basilica that Edgar Quinet summed up nicely in 1866: "A Janus-like monument with two faces, one turned to the past, the other to the future. Its name changes with the times."

To conceal the walls with bricked-up windows, Constant-Dufeux planned a decorative programme of paintings and sculptures dedicated to the life of Saint Geneviève and to the "great deeds of our nation's history". Unfortunately, the funds allocated proved to be insufficient. Whereas the Universal Exposition of 1867 was at full swing, the canons protested: "The altars are unseemly, the coverings are torn and let the planks show through, the tabernacles don't shut properly, the high altar is no longer sturdy. It is only in taking excessive care that we shall be able to decorate it on holidays." The only reminders of this period are the two groups of sculptures by Hippolyte Maindron placed under the peristyle: *Saint Geneviève Stopping Attila before Paris* in 1857 and *Clovis Being Baptised by Saint Remigius* in 1865. These works were moved in 1970.

1870: The Prussians attack

On 2 September 1870, the Second Empire collapsed and the Republic was proclaimed. But the situation was serious as the Prussian army was besieging Paris. Its shells pierced the dome of Sainte-Geneviève and damaged the vaulting. The crypt was used to store gunpowder and munitions.

While the National Assembly was drawing up the preliminaries of the peace treaty in Versailles, a revolutionary faction rebelled against the conditions imposed on France. On 18 March 1871, it formed the Paris Commune, which intended to take the place of the centralised government. The confrontation with regular troops, commanded by Mac-Mahon, was inevitable.

The Communards immediately took control of the basilica, flying the red flag over it. Harshly repressed, the insurrection ended in a bloodbath. On 26 May 1871, the Versailles artillery concentrated its fire on the basilica to force the insurgents to leave their shelter. One of them, the former deputy Jean-Baptiste Millière, editor of the newspaper *La Commune*, was taken prisoner. His conquerors made him kneel on the steps before shooting him. He died shouting: "Long live humanity!"

The last days of the church of Sainte-Geneviève

The fledgling Third Republic repaired the dome, reinforced the roofing, and even replaced the stone cross weighing a tonne and a half on top of the basilica! As the majority of the deputies in the National Assembly were Catholic and monarchist, Sainte-Geneviève remained a church. Marquis Philippe de Chennevières, then director of fine arts, was put in charge of establishing a decorative programme blending religious devotion and patriotism. He concocted a "vast poem of painting and sculpture" in praise of Saint Geneviève, patron saint of Paris, whose legend was combined with the history of the Christian roots of France. Although Abbot Bonnefoy, dean of the basilica, helped him choose the scenes to commission, Chennevières himself chose the artists, some of the most academic painters and sculptors of the period.

At the entrance of the nave, two panels evoked the life of Saint Denis. The cycle dedicated to Saint Geneviève occupied the walls of the central nave. The transept was devoted to the lives of Clovis, Charlemagne, Saint Louis, and Joan of Arc. The cul-de-four (half dome) of the apse was decorated with a mosaic, *Christ Showing the Angel of France the Destiny of Her People*. The portraitist Antoine Auguste Ernest Hébert produced the cartoons for it.

In May 1877, the public discovered the first murals by Puvis de Chavannes, *The Childhood of Saint Geneviève* and *The Meeting of Saint Geneviève and Saint Germanus*.

1885: A stone sponge cake for Victor Hugo

The decoration was finished in 1889. Unfortunately, it was yet again far too late for the basilica. For the monument had once again become a pantheon of the glories of the French Republic in 1885. The Third Republic, which had become markedly more radical, was responsible for the change. Henceforth, the most virulent advocated secularism. In 1879 the far-left deputy François Vincent Raspail strongly opposed the "chaplains chanting under the vault of the Panthéon", demanding that the monument be returned to its 1791 purpose. For several years, the debate raged in the Chamber.

The death of Victor Hugo, on 22 May 1885, put an end to it. The emotion aroused by the demise of the republican poet and senator was such that the government could decree that the building be returned to its civic function without giving rise to protests. His state funeral took place on 1 June. All of Europe sent floral wreaths. And all of Paris followed the nine-hour procession taking the author of *Les Misérables* to the entrance of "the finest ever sponge cake made of stone", as the writer had quipped before his death. At the time, he was unaware of the fact that he would be spending eternity there.

Henceforth dedicated to the "remains of the great men who merited the nation's gratitude", the monument became that of great national ceremonies, such as the centenary of the French Revolution. On this occasion, on 4 August 1889, Lazare Carnot, General Marceau, Jean-Baptiste Baudin, and Théophile Malo Corret de La Tour d'Auvergne were interred in the crypt. Corret de La Tour d'Auvergne took the place of General Hoche, whose descendants refused to have him buried there; they did not want their ancestor to be next to Carnot, who had him arrested for treason in 1794. On 22 September 1892, President Sadi Carnot celebrated the centenary of the proclamation of the Republic at the Panthéon. Two years later, he was assassinated in Lyon; he joined his grandfather in the crypt on 1 July 1894. He is still the only French president buried in the Panthéon.

Zola and Jaurès, heroes of the budding 20th century

The dawn of the 20th century was marked by a dispute: in 1906 the decision to transfer the ashes of the journalist and writer Émile Zola, ardent defender of Captain Dreyfus, brought the left, republican and socialist, into conflict with the right, fundamentally anti-Dreyfusard. The author of "J'accuse" ("I accuse") finally entered, two years later, on 4 June 1908. But the ceremony was disrupted by the journalist Grégori, who fired two shots inside the Panthéon, wounding in the arm Alfred Dreyfus, who had come to pay homage to his defender. Before that, in 1907, Marcellin Berthelot, a renowned chemist who also had been minister for education, then foreign minister, was interred in the monument. Léon Gambetta, hero of the siege of Paris in 1870, entered in 1920; the socialist deputy Jean Jaurès in 1924; and the mathematician and statesman Paul Painlevé in 1933. During the seventy years of the Third Republic, eleven personalities in total were interred in the Panthéon.

The grandiose funeral of Victor Hugo, 1 June 1885. Watercolour by Paul Sinibaldi, 19th century.

The Third Republic's final decorative touch

At the beginning of the 20th century, the decoration of the interior of the Panthéon had still not been finished, but the socialist Third Republic decided to finalise it. Despite its secular beliefs, it had the good sense not to touch the murals chosen by Chennevières. There was one exception: a composition dedicated to Notre-Dame de Lourdes was replaced by allegories (*Family*, *Nation*, *Fraternity*, and *The Divine Idea*).

In 1902 two places were still waiting for their painted decoration, including the apse that fell to Jean-Baptiste Édouard Detaille. Three years later, after having changed the theme twice, the artist delivered *Towards Glory*, a composition glorifying the armies of the French Republic. Also in 1905, Hector d'Espouy was commissioned for a forgotten bit of wall, the lunette above the entrance gallery, where he painted *Glory Entering the Temple*. He was the last artist to paint the walls of Panthéon.

But it was not until after the First World War that the colossal commissions of the pre-war years were executed. These hieratic stone and marble works reeled off the catechism of the Republic. Thus, in the choir, a grandiloquent monumental group by François Léon Sicard immortalised *The National Convention* (finished in 1921). In front of the piers of the transept crossing, there are four monuments: *To the Orators and Writers of the Restoration* by Laurent Honoré Marqueste, *To the Glory of the Generals of the Revolution* by Paul Jean-Baptiste Gasq, *To Jean-Jacques Rousseau* by Albert Bartholomé, and *To Diderot and the Encyclopedists* by Alphonse Camille Terroir. At the ends of the transept, two groups face each other: *To Unknown Heroes* by Louis Henri Bouchard and *To the Memory of Artists Whose Names Are Lost* by Paul Maximilien Landowski. In the nave, there are two evocations of the Revolution opposite each other: *Valmy* by Jules Desbois to the north and *The Avenger* by Ernest Dubois to the south. Of the thirty-seven initial commissions, only twenty or so works were executed. About a dozen are on site to this day. And of the series of great men, *Mirabeau* by Jean Antoine Injalbert still stands guard in the choir, accompanied by Jules Dalou's figure of *Hoche*.

B. 12. PARIS — Le Panthéon

The post-war years

The Third Republic came to an end during the Second World War. The Fourth Republic, which succeeded it, lasting from June 1944 to October 1958, did not go overboard with pantheonisations. It limited itself to five. In 1948 the physicist Paul Langevin, followed by another physicist Jean Perrin, founder of the Palais de la Découverte. In 1949 the colonial administrator Félix Éboué, one of the first to join the Free French; then Victor Schoelcher, the liberator of the slaves. On 22 June 1952, the remains of Louis Braille, inventor of the alphabet for the visually impaired, entered the Panthéon.

An observation airship flies over the Panthéon, early 20th century (private collection, Paris).

Under the Fifth Republic, General de Gaulle presided over the transfer of Jean Moulin's ashes on 19 December 1964. It was a grandiose ceremony. Marked by the funeral oration delivered by André Malraux, it celebrated the reunion of the Resistance fighters of the Second World War.

Seventeen years of sleep followed, until 21 May 1981: on the day of his inauguration, the new president of France, François Mitterrand, entered the Panthéon alone to leave a red rose on the graves of Jean Jaurès, Victor Schoelcher, and Jean Moulin, three defenders of human rights.

In 1987 René Cassin, winner of the Nobel Prize for Peace, was interred there; Jean Monnet, founder of the European Community, followed him in 1988. In 1989, for the bicentenary of the French Revolution, the remains of three revolutionary figures were transferred to the Panthéon: mathematician Gaspard Monge, Henri Grégoire, and the philosopher and mathematician Condorcet. In 1995 all of Europe watched with great emotion when the ashes of the physicists Pierre and Marie Curie were transferred to the Panthéon.

Under the presidency of Jacques Chirac, it was André Malraux, high priest of Gaullism, who was reunited with Jean Moulin in 1996. In 2002 he was joined with great pomp and ceremony by Alexandre Dumas.

Who will be the next to enter? That remains a mystery. But, while waiting, the Panthéon will not content itself with its role as a mausoleum. The eternal haven for great men is also a genuine museum of the history of France and—with its architecture, sculptures, and paintings—a vibrant homage to the arts.

On the evening of 30 November 2002, Alexandre Dumas entered the Panthéon under the protection of his beloved musketeers.

A closer look

Under the peristyle, brilliant light on the main door. Designed by Louis Nicolas Destouches, the three bronze doors were cast by Simonet *père et fils*.

Preceding pages

With its imposing dome rising above the rooftops of the Latin Quarter, the Panthéon seems to watch over Paris.

The Panthéon as seen from the windows of the law faculty. In the foreground, the pediment by David d'Angers dedicated to "the Nation distributing crowns handed to her by Liberty to great men, civil and military, while History inscribes their name". Four of the five bas-reliefs are visible between the columns of the peristyle.

AUX GRANDS HOMMES LA PATRIE RECONNAISSANTE

Detail of the left section, or the side where Liberty is depicted, of the pediment: the great men in the dress of the period look in the direction of the Nation. From right to left: Fénelon, his face in shadow; Monge; Mirabeau; and Malesherbes. Behind them are Laplace, Berthollet, Carnot, and Manuel, who is holding one of his lampoons. In the third group: La Fayette hidden by Cuvier, then David and his inseparable palette. Voltaire and Rousseau sit side by side; at their feet, the dying Bichat, then some students—the future elite of the nation. Not visible in this photograph, General Bonaparte is depicted on the right side of the pedimont.

AUX GRANDS HOMMES LA PAT

These two peristyle
bas-reliefs are the work of
the sculptor Charles François
Lebœuf, known as Nanteuil
(1792–1865): *The Apotheosis
of the Hero Who Died
for His Country* above
the lintel of the main door
and *The Judicature*.

The vault of the peristyle is a sumptuous backdrop against which the stone lacework of the laurel leaves of the capitals stands out.

A forest of Corinthian columns at sunset. In the background, the Bibliothèque Sainte-Geneviève.

Right-hand page

Since the lower windows were blocked up during the French Revolution, the blind façades have accentuated the severe aspect of the Panthéon, despite the frieze, a trace of Soufflot's decoration.

Invisible from the ground, the windows—and the flying buttresses and counterforts supporting the upper sections of the nave and transept—are concealed by an attic storey.

View of the Eiffel Tower
through the exterior colonnade
of the drum of the dome.

The dome's lantern
is a wonderful vantage
point over Paris.

Side view of the north arm of the transept with, on the east wall, the panels recounting the life of Joan of Arc. Despite being criticised for its cold style and conventional technique, the work by Jules Eugène Lenepveu (1819–1898) has made it into the history books. On the north wall, *Pro Patria*, or the civic virtues, by Jacques Ferdinand Humbert. The artist was inspired by Puvis de Chavannes, of whom he was a fervent admirer.

Joan of Arc before Orléans is the most famous painting in Lenepveu's series. A history painter, Lenepveu succeeded Paul Baudry, who died in 1886 before finishing the commission.

Saint Geneviève Providing for a Besieged Paris and *Saint Geneviève Watching over Paris* by Pierre Puvis de Chavannes (1824–1898), on the north wall of the choir. As Meissonier was in declining health in 1889, Puvis de Chavannes rose to the challenge, opting this time for cool shades of blue, grey, and white. According to legend, the artist was thinking of the blockade of Paris in 1870, when he painted the first theme, which covered three panels. Because of its extreme spareness, *Saint Geneviève Watching over Paris* remains the emblematic work of a painter who influenced both Symbolists and Nabis.

Christ Showing the Angel of France the Destiny of Her People by Antoine Auguste Ernest Hébert (1817–1908) decorates the cul-de-four (half dome) of the apse. To the angel's left, the artist has depicted Saint Geneviève prostrated and, to Christ's right, Joan of Arc, strapped into her armour, half-kneeling. An apologist for Italy, Hébert treated his subject in the manner of a Byzantine icon. It is the only decoration of the Panthéon executed in mosaic.

Towards Glory by Jean-Baptiste Édouard Detaille (1848–1912). When he was commissioned to decorate the apse in 1902, Detaille was an experienced artist, member of the Institut de France, and official painter of the army. He first thought about depicting Saint Geneviève and also considered an episode from *Les Trois Glorieuses*, then the departure of the volunteers of 1792, before opting for *Towards Glory*, a theme inspired by the composition he finished in the Hôtel de Ville: *Victory Leading the Armies of the Republic*. The powerful dynamism of this work is in stark contrast with the rest of the decoration. The battle painter's palette of warm colours exalts the heroism of the armies riding towards the heavens.

The Death of Saint Geneviève by Jean-Paul Laurens (1838–1921), on the south wall of the choir. At the height of his fame, the artist spent eleven years working on this commission, choosing to dedicate the triptych to the death of the saint and the single panel to her funeral. The artist's pungent realism gave rise to criticism. There is nothing religious about the painting: a woman dies, surrounded by a disparate crowd.

The Baptism of Clovis by Paul Joseph Blanc. This is the fourth panel of the cycle dedicated to Clovis. After the victory at Tolbiac, the king of the Franks was baptised by the bishop of Reims, Saint Remigius, in a setting that is curiously like that of the Panthéon.

Left-hand page

The Battle of Tolbiac by Paul Joseph Blanc (1846–1904). This large painting is a little cold but well suited to the space, which forms an attractive group located on the east wall of the south arm of the transept. Like most of the artists, Blanc decorated four panels and their friezes, separated by engaged columns. But the commission required that each theme be treated in two compositions: one on three panels, the other on a single panel.

The Miracles of Saint Geneviève by Théodore Maillot (1826–1888), south arm of the transept. This theme was treated by the artist in the style of the painted manuscripts of the Middle Ages. The two panels represent the procession of the reliquary of Saint Geneviève organised in 1496 to bring an end to the torrential rain and flooding. The bishop of Paris, depicted under a canopy, bears a surprising resemblance to Mgr Guibert, who was archbishop of Paris in 1871.

Right-hand page

The Meeting of Saint Geneviève and Saint Germanus and Saint Loup by Pierre Puvis de Chavannes. On the south wall of the nave, this composition of three panels belongs to the cycle dedicated to the childhood of Saint Geneviève. This serene work, which corresponds to the turning point of the artist's career, heralds the beginnings of the monumental mural art of which he was the initiator.

LE MARTYRE DE SAINT DENIS

The Martyrdom of Saint Denis by Joseph Florentin Léon Bonnat (1833–1922). This work, which decorates the north wall of the first bay of the nave, is the pendant to The Sermon of Saint Denis by Pierre Victor Galland (1822–1892) on the south wall. Treated in the style of an ancient tragedy, this painting, which is reproduced in French history textbooks, is one of the best-known in the Panthéon.

Right-hand page

The March of Attila by Jules Élie Delaunay (1828–1891) is located on the north side of the nave. It is the fourth part of the cycle dedicated to the theme of Saint Geneviève calming the Parisians menaced by Attila's Huns. Rejecting any claim to realism, Delaunay proposes a poetic vision of this tragic episode in the history of Paris.

The Life of Saint Louis by Alexandre Cabanel (1823–1889) decorates the west wall of the north arm of the transept. The favourite painter of the court of Napoleon III and a renowned portraitist, he did not respect the rules imposed on the artists. He chose to depict the life of Louis IX in three scenes: Saint Louis taught by his mother, dispensing justice, and prisoner in Palestine.

ST LOUIS REND LA JUSTICE ABOLIT
LES COMBATS JUDICIAIRES FONDE LES
INSTITUTIONS QUI ONT FAIT SA GLOIRE

Interior view of the Panthéon: the lovely arrangement of vaults and columns comprises a neo-classical decor evoking Soufflot's Italian influences. The republican statuary is the only jarring note in the harmonious aesthetics of the place. From left to right: *Valmy* by Jules Desbois (1851–1935) with its confused composition; *To the Orators and Writers of the Restoration*, a stilted work by Laurent Honoré Marqueste (1848–1920); the grandiloquent *National Convention* by François Léon Sicard (1862–1934); *To the Glory of the Generals of the Revolution* by Paul Jean-Baptiste Gasq (1860–1944) in which General Bonaparte is depicted on horseback; and *The Avenger* by Ernest Dubois (1863–1930), an evocation of the heroic end of the sailors of *Le Vengeur du people* (The Avenger of the People), a ship sunk by the British on 1 June 1794.

The Avenger, marble group
by Ernest Dubois
(1863–1930). This sculpture
evoked the heroic end of
Le Vengeur du peuple
(The Avenger of the People)
during the naval battle with
British vessels on 13 Prairial,
Year II (1 June 1794);
260 of the 723 men making
up the crew were captured
by the British.

To Unknown Heroes by Louis
Henri Bouchard (1875–1960),
south arm of the transept.
Delayed by the First World
War, the artist changed his
project in order to depict
soldiers. Under the allegories
of Glory and Memory holding
hands are the bodies of the
unknown heroes and, at the
bottom, the recumbent effigy
of a *poilu*.

Right-hand page

*To Diderot and the
Encyclopedists* by Alphonse
Camille Terroir (1875–1955),
north-west pier of the
transept crossing. At the foot
of an obelisk are two hieratic
women flanked by allegories
of Truth and Strength.
Below, the profile of Diderot
decorates a tomb,
which breaks the harmony
of the group.

*To the Glory of the Generals
of the Revolution* by
Paul Jean-Baptiste Gasq
(1860–1944), south-east pier
of the transept crossing.
Below an obelisk decorated
with an allegory of
the Republic and flags
are the generals. The group
is of no real interest apart
from the presence of
Bonaparte on horseback.

A LA GLOIRE
DES GÉNÉRAUX
DE LA
RÉVOLUTION FRANÇAISE

At the transept crossing, view of the north-west pier: on the floor, the monument *To Diderot and the Encyclopedists*, executed by Alphonse Camille Terroir (1875–1955) in the pared-down style of the 1920s. Above is one of the four pendentives painted by Gérard; this one depicts Glory welcoming Napoleon who is wearing the imperial mantle.

Above the north-east pier, a pendentive featuring an allegory of Death. The skilfully controlled lunar lighting in this work by Gérard heralded Romanticism.

Evidence of the religious nature of the building, this frieze, which runs along the lintels of the nave, had been commissioned by Soufflot. Decorated with roses (immortality and the Virgin Mary), vines (the Eucharist), and ears of corn (the Resurrection), it was spared by Quatremère de Quincy.

Interior decorations from the revolutionary period are rare. Only the four small pendentives of the oval cupola of the entrance nave, above the organ loft, remain. These winged animals— emblems of the Genius of the Arts (the swan), Philosophy (the eagle), the Sciences (the cockerel), and Virtue (the pelican)— replaced a concert of musician angels.

The cupola, as it appears to visitors. The four pendentives—*Glory*, *Death*, *The Nation*, and *Justice*—painted by François Gérard (1770–1837), enhance the vivid colours in the fresco by Gros. Gérard died on the job, which was finished by his pupils Mlle Godefroid and the Italian Carmeli.

The Apotheosis of Saint Geneviève by Antoine Jean Gros (1771–1835). Napoleon I was at the height of his fame in 1811, when Gros was commissioned to paint the cupola. A sketch reveals that he planned to paint four groups: Clovis and Clotilde, founders of the original church; Charlemagne and Hildegard; Saint Louis and Queen Marguerite with a Crusaders' standard as a backdrop; and Napoleon I, wearing a laurel wreath, and Empress Marie-Louise holding the young king of Rome.
The fall of the Empire, the fledgling Restoration, and the Hundred Days called the work into question. The imperial family was replaced by Louis XVIII, his niece, the duchess of Angoulême, and the new heir, the young duke of Bordeaux. Gros also replaced the church of Sainte-Geneviève with a representation of the patron saint seated on a rock. Unveiled by Charles X on 4 November 1824, the work earned the artist the title of baron.

Interior of the dome: view of the three superposed calottes with the cast-iron bridge installed by the architect Louis Pierre Baltard to attain the fresco by Baron Gros.

Deaf to the criticisms that the work was difficult to see from ground level, Gros retorted that his paintings were meant to be looked at up close. From left to right: Queen Marguerite and Saint Louis pointing to the Crown of Thorns, and Hildegard and Charlemagne.

Right-hand page

The unseen side of the dome confirms Soufflot's boldness in unveiling the architectural beauty of the third calotte. The staircase straddling the second cupola leads to the lantern.

The secrets of the Panthéon:
above the cupolas of
the nave at the junction
of the dome, a winding
barrel vault and one
of the many wooden winches
used to move the chandeliers
up and down.

A ring of vaults around
the base of the dome: iron
rods and tie beams make up
a metallic structure
reinforcing the framework.

Near the entrance is a series
of powerful Doric columns,
reminiscent of those
of the Temple of Neptune
in Paestum that Soufflot
had so admired during
his travels in Italy.

In the west gallery of the crypt, four bronze plaques honouring the victims of the revolutions of 1830 and 1848.

Exiled to the old abbey of Sainte-Geneviève before its demolition, saved from the revolutionary purge by Quatremère de Quincy, Soufflot's tomb took its place in the east crypt of the Panthéon, beside Voltaire, on 19 February 1829.

The impressive central core of the network of the galleries in the crypt, which form a cross-shaped plan similar to the upper part of the building.

Another of the secret places of the Panthéon, this gallery, which has no reason to be envious of Vauban's forts, forms a tight circle around the crypt.

The tomb of Jean-Jacques Rousseau is in the form of an ancient temple from which emerges a hand, brandishing the torch of philosophy (east gallery of the crypt).

In the same gallery, opposite Rousseau, the tomb of Voltaire is topped by the blue sphere of the earth; in front of it is a standing sculpture of the philosopher by Houdon.

President Sadi Carnot, assassinated in 1894, rests beside his grandfather, Lazare Carnot, in vault XXIII, which also contains the graves of Corret de La Tour d'Auvergne and General Marceau. He is the only president of the French Republic buried in the Panthéon.

Top left

The tomb of Marshal Lannes in vault XXII. Mortally wounded at the Battle of Essling, on 21 May 1809, he died in Napoleon's arms on 31 May. He is the only marshal of the Empire buried in the Panthéon.

Only the heart of Léon Gambetta rests in a porphyry urn between two republican lictors' fasces, located in a niche near the east staircase. The transfer took place on 11 November 1920, the same day as the burial of the Unknown Soldier under the Arc de Triomphe.

In depth

Foucault's pendulum

In 1851 Louis Napoleon Bonaparte, the prince-president who was keen on science and history, granted the physicist Léon Foucault permission to use the dome of the Panthéon to pursue his experiments on the rotation of the Earth. With the help of the engineer Gustave Froment, Foucault set up a 28-kilogram pendulum, suspended from a 67-metre-long steel wire, there. On the floor, a large mahogany circle centred on the vertical line of the point of suspension defined the oscillation space, which was covered with small mounds of fine sand. The experiment began on 31 March. Foucault observed that with every swing, the stylus attached to the bottom of the pendulum made a groove in the sand that progressively got larger. It was the first material proof of the movement of the Earth.

The success of the demonstration attracted many visitors, at which the Catholic party took umbrage. Careful not to ruffle the feathers of a favourable electorate, Louis Napoleon put an end to the experiment on 1 December 1851.

In 1902 Camille Flammarion, founder of the Société Astronomique de France, voiced the wish to repeat Foucault's experiment—which was interrupted by the coup d'état of 2 December 1851, "before all the conclusions were drawn"—under the dome. It was easy for him to obtain permission because the Panthéon was henceforth a secular monument.

The inaugural session took place on 22 October 1902. Over two thousand people attended, including Camille Saint-Saëns, Rodin, Bartholdi, and the descendants of Léon Foucault. A silk ribbon held back the pendulum. Joseph Chaumié, minister for education and fine arts, held a lit match to it, burning it and thus freeing the pendulum, which began to oscillate. It was a great success!

The experiment ended on 23 July 1903, but 92 years later, in October 1995, the Caisse Nationale des Monuments Historiques et des Sites, in association with the Musée du Conservatoire National des Arts et Métiers (CNAM), repeated it on the occasion of *Science en fête*, an annual celebration of science. Using Froment's ball, engineers observed oscillation times that were more or less identical to those of the 1851 experiment.

In 1 July 1996, Froment's ball once again became part of the CNAM collections, but another sphere, designed by the engineer Jacques Foiret, succeeded it. Since then, it has continued to oscillate under the inquisitive gaze of visitors to the Panthéon.

The experiment of Foucault's pendulum made the front page of the newspaper *Le Petit Parisien* on 2 November 1902.

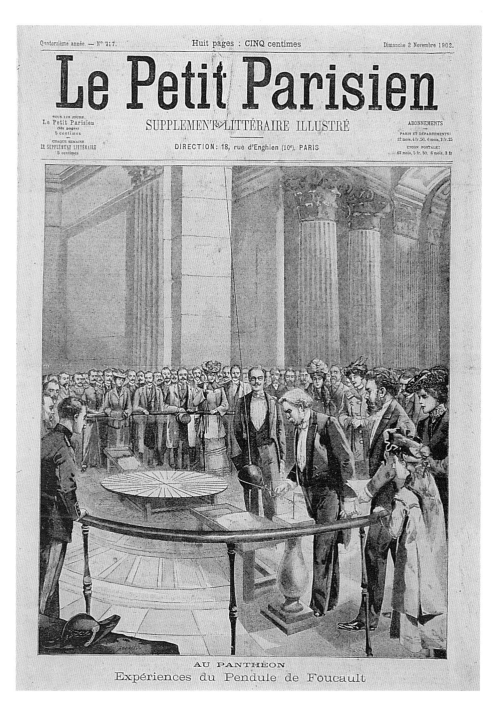

AU PANTHÉON
Expériences du Pendule de Foucault

The worthies of the crypt

Vault XXIV, the tombs of Victor Hugo, on the left; Émile Zola, on the right; and Alexandre Dumas, at the back.

Émile Zola's entrance into the Panthéon on 4 June 1908 did not meet with unanimous approval. Subversive postcard of the time (BHVP, Paris).

Seventy-two people are currently buried in the necropolis, including the wife of Marcellin Berthelot, the father of Victor Schoelcher, and the architect Soufflot, who were admitted without a decree being passed.

1791

Honoré Gabriel Riqueti, count of Mirabeau (1749–1791), deputy. Removed in 1794.
François Marie Arouet, known as Voltaire (1694–1778), writer.

1792

Nicolas Joseph Beaurepaire (1740–1792), soldier. Never transferred.

1793

Louis Michel Lepeletier de Saint-Fargeau (1760–1793), deputy. His remains were returned to his family in 1795.
Auguste Henri Marie Picot, marquis of Dampierre (1756–1793), soldier. Never transferred.

1794

Jean-Paul Mara, known as Marat (1743–1793), doctor, journalist, and deputy. Removed in 1795.
Jean-Jacques Rousseau (1712–1778), writer.

1806

François Denis Tronchet (1726–1806), jurist, senator.
Claude Louis Petiet (1749–1806), deputy, minister, senator, grand officer of the Legion of Honour.

1807

Jean-Baptiste Pierre Bévière (1723–1807), notary, deputy, senator.
Louis Joseph Charles Amable d'Albert, duke of Luynes (1748–1807), soldier, deputy, senator. His remains were returned to his family in 1862.
Jean Étienne Marie Portalis (1746–1807), jurist, minister.
Louis-Pierre Pantaléon Resnier (1759–1807), man of letters, senator.

1808

Antoine César de Choiseul, duke of Praslin (1756–1808), soldier, deputy, senator.

Jean-Frédéric Perrégaux (1744–1808), banker.

Jean-Pierre Firmin, Count Malher (1761–1808), general. Only his heart is buried in the crypt.
Pierre Jean Georges, Count Cabanis (1757–1808), doctor, aesthete, senator. His remains, but not his heart, are buried in the crypt.
François Barthélemy Béguignot, known as Count Béguinot (1747–1808), general, deputy, senator.
Gabriel Louis, marquis of Caulaincourt (1741–1808), general, senator. His remains, but not his heart, are buried in the crypt.

1809

Girolamo Luigi Francesco Maria, Count Durazzo (1739–1809), last doge of Genoa, senator. Only his heart is buried in the crypt.
Jean-Baptiste Papin, count of Saint-Christau (1756–1809), lawyer, deputy, senator.
Joseph Marie, Count Vien (1716–1809), painter, David's teacher, senator.

Pierre Garnier, count of La Boissière (1755–1809), general, senator, grand officer of the Legion of Honour.
Justin Bonaventure, Count Morard de Galles (1741–1809), admiral, senator, grand officer of the Legion of Honour. Only his heart is buried in the crypt.
Jean-Pierre, Count Sers (1746–1809), senator. Only his heart is buried in the crypt.
Emmanuel Crétet, count of Champmol (1747–1809), governor of the Banque de France, minister of the interior. His remains, but not his heart or viscera, are buried in the crypt.

1810

Louis Vincent Joseph Le Blond, count of Saint-Hilaire (1766–1809), general, grand eagle of the Legion of Honour. His funeral took place at the church of Sainte-Geneviève, together with that of Marshal Lannes.
Jean Lannes, duke of Montebello (1769–1809), marshal of France. The only one of

Napoleon I's marshals to be buried in the Panthéon.
Giovanni Battista, Cardinal Caprara (1733–1810), papal legate to Paris, senator.
Charles Pierre Claret, count of Fleurieu (1738–1810), naval minister, councillor of state, senator.
Jean-Baptiste, Count Treilhard (1742–1810), lawyer, councillor of state, legislator, grand officer of the Legion of Honour.

1811

Nicolas Marie, Count Songis des Courbons (1761–1810), general, grand eagle of the Legion of Honour.
Charles, Cardinal Erskine of Kellie (1739–1811). He was held captive with Pius VII in Fontainebleau. His funeral took place at the church of Saint-Thomas-d'Aquin, at the same time as that of Cardinal Mareri.
Ippolito Antonio Vicente, Cardinal Mareri (1738–1811). He blessed the union of Napoleon I and Archduchess Marie-Louise on 2 April 1810. Claimed by Rome, his remains were exhumed on 22 August 1861.
Alexandre-Antoine Hureau, baron of Sénarmont (1769–1810), general. Only his heart is buried in the crypt.
Michel Ortner, count, known as Ordener (1755–1811), general, senator, governor of the Palais de Compiègne.
Louis Antoine, count of Bougainville (1729–1811), navigator, senator, grand officer

of the Legion of Honour. Only his body is buried in the crypt.

1812

Jan Willem de Winter (1761–1812), marshal of the Netherlands. Only his body is buried in the crypt.
Jean Marie Pierre François Doursenne, Count Le Paige, known as Dorsenne (1776–1812), general, grand officer of the Legion of Honour.

1813

Joseph-Louis Lagrangia, Count Lagrange (1736–1813), mathematician, senator, grand officer of the Legion of Honour.
Jean Jacques Ignace Jacqueminot, count of Ham (1754–1813), lawyer, deputy, senator.
Hyacinthe Hugues Timoléon, count of Brissac, duke of Cossé (1746–1813), senator.
François Marie Joseph Justin, count of Viry (1737–1813), senator.
Jean, Count Rousseau (1738–1813), senator. Only his body is buried in the crypt.

1814

Jean Nicolas, Count Démeunier (1751–1814), senator, grand officer of the Legion of Honour.
Jean Louis Ebénézer, Count Reynier (1771–1814), general.
Claude Ambroise Regnier, duke of Massa (1736–1814), deputy, councillor of state, minister, grand officer of the Legion of Honour.
Frederik Henry, Count Walther (1761–1813), general.

1815

Claude Juste Alexandre Louis, Count Legrand (1762–1815), general, senator, grand eagle of the Legion of Honour.
Antoine Jean Marie, Count Thévenard (1733–1815), vice-admiral, senator, grand officer of the Legion of Honour.

1829

Jacques Germain Soufflot (1713–1780), architect. Buried in his masterpiece according to the wishes of the *génovéfains*.

1885

Victor Hugo (1802–1885), writer, peer of France, deputy, senator.

1889

Théophile-Malo Corret de La Tour d'Auvergne (1743–1800), officer.
Lazare Nicolas Marguerite, Count Carnot (1753–1823), general, deputy, minister, scholar.
Jean-Baptiste Alphonse Victor Baudin (1811–1851), doctor, deputy.
François Séverin Marceau-Desgraviers, known as Marceau (1769–1796), general.

1894

Marie François Sadi Carnot (1837–1894), engineer, president of the French Republic.

1907

Pierre Eugène Marcellin Berthelot (1827–1907), chemist, senator, minister. He was buried with his wife Sophie Berthelot (1837–1907), who died a few

hours before him. She was the first woman interred in the crypt.

1908

Émile Édouard Charles Antoine Zola (1840–1902), writer.

1920

Léon Michel Gambetta (1838–1882), lawyer, politician. Only his heart is buried in the crypt, in a porphyry urn between two lictors' fasces.

1924

Jean Jaurès (1859–1914), politician, journalist.

1933

Paul Painlevé (1863–1933), mathematician, politician.

1948

Paul Langevin (1872–1946), physicist.
Jean Baptiste Perrin (1870–1942), physicist, 1926 Nobel Prize for Physics.

1949

Félix Adolphe Sylvestre Éboué (1884–1944), colonial administrator, Compagnon

Plaque to the memory of Antoine de Saint-Exupéry, who died on a mission on 31 July 1944. The plaque was unveiled against the south pier of the transept crossing on 17 September 1965. His names also figures among the 197 "Writers who died in combat for France".

de la Libération, Citation
à l'Ordre de la Nation.
Victor Schoelcher (1804–1893),
politician. Buried, according
to his wishes, with his father,
Marc Schoelcher (1766–1832).

1952

Louis Simon Braille (1809–1852),
inventor of the Braille method.
His body is buried in the crypt
and an urn containing his hands
is in the family tomb in
Coupvray, Seine-et-Marne.

1964

Jean Moulin (1899–1943),
Resistance fighter,
Compagnon de la Libération.

1987

René Cassin (1887–1976), jurist,
Compagnon de la Libération,
1968 Nobel Prize for Peace.

1988

Jean Monnet (1888–1979),
economist, politician, nicknamed
"the father of Europe".

1989

Marie Jean Antoine Nicolas
de Caritat, marquis of Condorcet
(1743–1794), philosopher,
mathematician, deputy.
Henri Baptiste Grégoire, known
as Abbé Grégoire (1750–1831),
clergyman and politician.
Gaspard Monge, count of Péluse
(1746–1818), mathematician,
deputy, senator.

1995

Pierre Curie (1859–1906)
and Marie Sklodowska Curie
(1867–1934), physicists, 1903
Nobel Prize for Physics. Marie
Curie also received the Nobel
Prize for Chemistry in 1911.

1996

Georges André Malraux
(1901–1976), writer, politician,
Compagnon de la Libération.

2002

Alexandre Davy de La Pailleterie,
known as Alexandre Dumas
(1802–1870), writer.

The honours of the Panthéon

On 29 July 1831, Louis-Philippe
paid homage to the insurgents
of *Les Trois Glorieuses* by
unveiling four bronze tablets
bearing the names of the heroes
of July 1830 in the central
corridor of the crypt. The king
of the French had just made
the Panthéon a place of memory
in which the glorious dead were
honoured without, however,
being buried in the crypt
(see page 53).
The list of victims got longer
after the two world wars:
560 writers died in combat
during the First World War;
197 writers died in combat
during the Second World War.
And on 18 January 2007,
President Jacques Chirac,
accompanied by Simone Veil,
president of the Fondation
pour la Mémoire de la Shoah,
in the presence of 200 surviving
"Righteous", unveiled the
plaque dedicated to
the 2,725 French "Righteous
among the Nations".
There are also memorial
plaques, including those of
the philosopher Henri Bergson;
General Delestraint, who died
in Dachau; and two emblematic
heroes, Georges Guynemer
and Antoine de Saint-Exupéry.

Vigil in front of the coffin
of André Malraux,
23 November 1996.

The architects

Jacques Germain Soufflot
(1713–1780)

A vocation for drawing and architecture encouraged this son of a Burgundian notary to make his first trip to Italy. Pulling strings, he got a place at the Académie de France in Rome, where he studied the architecture of domed churches. Back in France, he worked to smarten up Lyon before conquering Paris thanks to the support of the duke of Villeroy and the marquis of Marigny. Appointed intendant of the king's buildings in 1755, he was ennobled the following year.

A real man of the Enlightenment, the confirmed bachelor was close to the Freemasons. The *Mercure de France* newspaper saw in him "the Bernini of our times".

Maximilien Brébion
(1716–1792)

Soufflot hired him as "principal partner" for the Panthéon building project. Brébion took over from Soufflot in 1780, working with Rondelet and Soufflot's nephew. He built the Marché Sainte-Catherine in the Marais district of Paris in 1786.

Antoine Chrysostome Quatremère de Quincy
(1755–1848)

A sculptor with a passion for architecture, he travelled all over Italy and England to study monuments. His reflections enriched his *Dictionnaire d'architecture* (1788). The Convention put him in charge of the Panthéon until 1794, but he worked with Brébion and Rondelet.

Jean-Baptiste Rondelet
(1743–1829)

The son of a master mason from Lyon, he started working for Soufflot in 1770 as a draughtsman. Engaged for the church of Sainte-Geneviève building project, he was in charge of the "mechanics of the construction". He saved Soufflot's work, using all sorts of remedies to reinforce it, making him the inventor of "prestressed masonry". The author of a *Traité théorique et pratique de l'art de bâtir* (Theoretical and Practical Treatise of the Art of Building), he spent his last years, blind and infirm, near the Panthéon.

Louis Pierre Baltard
(1764–1846)

A landscape engraver, the artist chose to go into architecture after a trip to Italy. A neoclassical architect and professor at the École Polytechnique and then the École des Beaux-Arts, he was appointed to work on the Panthéon on 14 April 1813. He dreamed of making it the

"Vatican of the Gauls", but many of his projects (pediment, lantern, monumental entrance) came to nothing.

Nicolas Destouches
(1789–1850)

The architect, who succeeded Baltard during the July Monarchy, carried out work that had already been planned, such as the creation of railings to surround the entire building. He tried to adapt to the successive political systems.

Simon Claude Constant-Dufeux
(1801–1870)

The grandson of a master mason who worked on the church of Sainte-Geneviève under Soufflot, he succeeded Destouches in 1850. He was supposed to make the Panthéon a national basilica on a shoestring. His ambitious projects to enrich Soufflot's work were mothballed. He executed the bronze decoration of the side doors.

Caricature of Quatremère de Quincy, in *Album de 73 portraits-charge aquarellés* by Louis Léopold Boilly. Manuscript, 19th century (Bibliothèque de l'Institut, Paris).

Left
Jacques Germain Soufflot by Louis Michel Van Loo, oil on canvas, 18th century (Musée du Louvre, Paris).

Louis Pierre Baltard by Jean-Baptiste Claude Guillaume Eugène, plaster, 1873 (Musée d'Orsay, Paris).

Centre des monuments nationaux

President
Isabelle Lemesle

Publishing director
Dominique Seridji

Publications coordinator
Clair Morizet

Assistant publications coordinator
Karin Franques

Editorial and documentation coordinator
Anne-Sophie Grouhel-Le Tellec

Translator
Chrisoula Petridis

Copy editor
Susan Schneider

Graphic design and layout
Régis Dutreuil

Production coordinator
Carine Merse

Photoengraving
JOUVE Orléans, Saran

Printing
IME, Baume-les-Dames, France

Abbreviations

BNF: Bibliothèque Nationale de France
CMN: Centre des monuments nationaux
MAP: Médiathèque de l'Architecture et du Patrimoine

© Éditions du patrimoine
Centre des monuments nationaux
Paris, 2010
Dépôt légal: October 2010
ISBN: 978-2-7577-0090-7

Acknowledgements

The author and the Éditions du patrimoine would like to extend their warm thanks to the administrator of the Panthéon and his team for the kind interest they have shown in this project.

Photographic credits

CMN/Bernard Acloque: 10, 11, 47
CMN/Philippe Berthé: 7bl, 60bl
CMN/Patrick Cadet: 29, 31, 32b
CMN/Jean-Jacques Hautefeuille: 5
CMN/Pascal Lemaître: 27l, 62
CMN/Alain Lonchampt: 7br
CMN/Jean-Luc Paillé: 2, 44
CMN/Caroline Rose: front cover, 6, 7t, 14, 17, 18–19, 20, 21, 22, 23, 24, 25, 26, 27tr, 28, 29, 30, 32t, 33, 34, 35, 36, 37, 38, 39, 40–41, 42, 43, 45, 46, 48, 49, 50, 51, 52, 53, 54, 55, 56, 57, 58, 60tr, 61
RMN/Christian Jean: 63tl
RMN (Institut de France)/Gérard Blot: 63tr
RMN (Musée d'Orsay)/Hervé Lewandowski: 63br
Shortcut Events: 16

Illustrations, cover, and opening pages

Front cover: A few hundred metres from the clock tower of Saint-Étienne-du-Mont, the Panthéon emerges from the rooftops of Paris.

Page 17: To prevent the drums of the columns being chipped during construction, the builders left small cubes—*mains*—jutting out, which enabled the drums to be hung from the ropes of the crane. The protruding cubes were later sawn off the shafts, before the fluting was carved.

Page 58: Unexpectedly... the Panthéon.